Wombats

Julie Murray

Abdo
NOCTURNAL ANIMALS
Kids

abdopublishing.com

Published by Abdo Kids, a division of ABDO, PO Box 398166, Minneapolis, Minnesota 55439.
Printed in the United States of America, North Mankato, Minnesota.

102017

012018

 THIS BOOK CONTAINS
RECYCLED MATERIALS

Photo Credits: Alamy, Glow Images, iStock, Minden Pictures, Shutterstock

Production Contributors: Teddy Borth, Jennie Forsberg, Grace Hansen

Design Contributors: Christina Doffing, Candice Keimig, Dorothy Toth

Publisher's Cataloging-in-Publication Data

Names: Murray, Julie, author.

Title: Wombats / by Julie Murray.

Description: Minneapolis, Minnesota : Abdo Kids, 2018. | Series: Nocturnal animals |
        Includes glossary, index and online resource (page 24).

Identifiers: LCCN 2017908181 | ISBN 9781532104091 (lib.bdg.) | ISBN 9781532105210 (ebook) |
        ISBN 9781532105777 (Read-to-me ebook)

Subjects: LCSH: Wombats--Juvenile literature. | Nocturnal animals--Juvenile literature. |
        Endemic animals--Australia--Juvenile literature.

Classification: DDC 599.2--dc23

LC record available at https://lccn.loc.gov/2017908181

Table of Contents

Wombats

Wombats live in Australia.

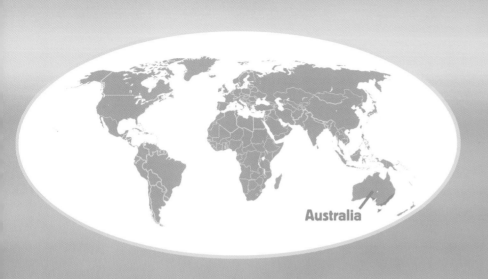

Australia

They have small eyes and ears.

They have short legs. They have short tails too.

They have **fur**. It can be any shade of brown.

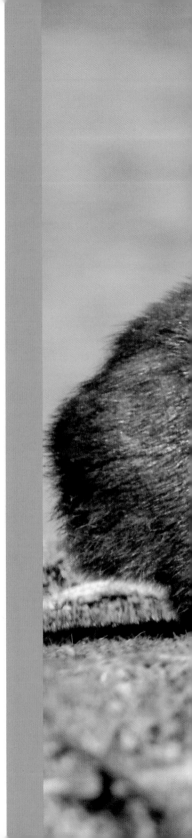

They have sharp claws.

They use them to dig.

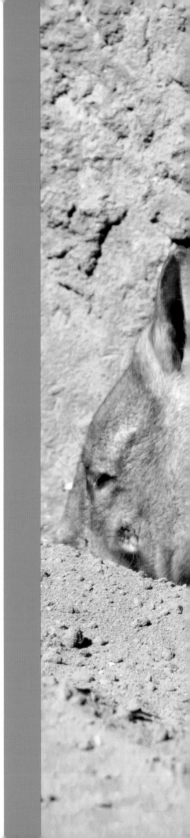

12

Wombats rest in **burrows**.

They sleep during the day.

They come out at night.

They are ready to eat!

They only eat plants. They eat grass. They like roots too.

The young grow in a **pouch**.

They drink their mother's milk.

Features of Wombats

sharp claws

short legs

short tail

small ears

Glossary

burrow
a hole or tunnel dug by a small animal.

pouch
a stomach pocket where some animals carry their young.

fur
usually the short, fine, soft hair of some animals. However, a wombat has rough, thick fur.

Index

Abdo Kids ONLINE
FREE! ONLINE MULTIMEDIA RESOURCES

Visit **abdokids.com** and use this code to access crafts, games, videos, and more!

Abdo Kids Code:
NWK4091